Samuel Cooper

A Sermon Preached Before His Excellency John Hancock, esq

Governour, the honourable the Senate, and House of representatives of

the commonwealth of Massachusetts, October 25, 1780.

Samuel Cooper

A Sermon Preached Before His Excellency John Hancock, esq
Governour, the honourable the Senate, and House of representatives of the
commonwealth of Massachusetts, October 25, 1780.

ISBN/EAN: 9783337213770

Printed in Europe, USA, Canada, Australia, Japan

Cover: Foto ©Lupo / pixelio.de

More available books at **www.hansebooks.com**

COO...

M

ON · TH...

...ENC...

OF · TH...

Conſtitution, &c.

SERMON

PREACHED BEFORE HIS EXCELLENCY

JOHN HANCOCK, Esq;

GOVERNOUR,

THE HONOURABLE THE

SENATE,

AND

HOUSE OF REPRESENTATIVES,

OF THE

COMMONWEALTH

OF

MASSACHUSETTS,

OCTOBER 25, 1780.

BEING THE DAY OF THE
COMMENCEMENT OF THE CONSTITUTION,
AND
INAUGURATION OF THE NEW GOVERNMENT.

By SAMUEL COOPER, D.D.

COMMONWEALTH OF MASSACHUSETTS:
PRINTED BY T. AND J. FLEET, AND J. GILL.

In the Houſe of Repreſentatives, June 24, 1780.

ORDERED, That Colonel *Dawes* and Major *Oſgood*, with ſuch as the Honourable Board ſhall join, be a Committee to inform the Rev. Dr. Cooper that the two Houſes have made choice of him to preach a Sermon on the laſt Wedneſday of October next, being the firſt Day of General Election under the new Conſtitution.

Sent up for Concurrence,
JOHN HANCOCK, Speaker;

In Council, June 4, 1780,
Read and concurred, and *Thomas Cuſhing*, Eſq; is joined.
JOHN AVERY, Dep. Secr'y.
Conſented to by the Major Part of the Council.
A true Copy,
Atteſt. JOHN AVERY, Dep. Secr'y.

The Commonwealth of Maſſachuſetts.

In the Houſe of Repreſentatives, October 26, 1780.

ORDERED, That Mr. *Lowell* and Col. *Dawes* be appointed a Committee, with ſuch as the Honourable Senate ſhall join, to wait on the Rev. Doct. Cooper and return him the Thanks of both Houſes for his Sermon Yeſterday delivered before the General Aſſembly, and to requeſt a Copy thereof for the Preſs.

Sent up for Concurrence,
CALEB DAVIS, Speaker.

In Senate, October 30, 1780.
Read and concurred, and *Abraham Fuller*, Eſq; is joined on the part of the Senate.
THOMAS CUSHING, Preſident,
True Copy,
Atteſt. JOHN AVERY, Secr'y.

A

SERMON, &c.

XXXth JEREMIAH, 20, 21 Ver.

" Their Congregation fhall
" be eftablifhed before me:
" and their Nobles fhall be
" of themfelves, and their
" Governor fhall proceed
" from the midft of them."

NOTHING can be more applicable
to the folemnity in which we are
engaged, than this paffage of
facred writ. The Prophecy feems to have
been made for ourfelves, it is fo exactly
defcriptive of that important, that compre-
henfive, that effential civil bleffing, which
kindles the luftre, and diffufes the joy of
the prefent day. Nor is this the only

B   paffage

paſſage of holy Scripture that holds up to our view a ſtriking reſemblance between our own circumſtances and thoſe of the antient Iſraelites ; a nation choſen by God a theatre for the diſplay of ſome of the moſt aſtoniſhing diſpenſations of his Providence. Like that nation we roſe from oppreſſion, and emerged " from the Houſe of Bondage": Like that nation we were led into a wilderneſs, as a refuge from tyranny, and a preparation for the enjoyment of our civil and religious rights : Like that nation we have been purſued through the ſea, by the armed hand of power, which, but for the ſignal interpoſitions of Heaven, muſt before now have totally defeated the noble purpoſe of our emigration : And, to omit many other inſtances of ſimilarity, like that nation we have been ungrateful to the Supreme Ruler of the world, and too " lightly eſteemed the Rock of our Salvation"; accordingly, we have been corrected by his juſtice, and at the ſame time remarkably ſupported and defended by his mercy : So that we may diſcern our own picture in the figure of the antient church divinely exhibited to Moſes in viſion, " a buſh burning and not conſumed." This day, this memorable day, is a witneſs, that the Lord, He whoſe
" hand

" hand maketh great, and giveth ftrength unto all, hath not forfaken us, nor our God forgotten us." This day, which forms a new æra in our annals, exhibits a teftimony to all the world, that contrary to our deferts, and amidft all our troubles, the blefling promifed in our text to the afflicted feed of Abraham is come upon us; "Their Nobles fhall be of themfelves, and their Governor fhall proceed from the midft of them."

This Prophecy has an immediate refpect to the deliverance of the Jews from the cruel oppreffions of the king of Babylon. Their fufferings, when they fell under the power of this haughty tyrant, as they are reprefented to us in facred hiftory, muft harrow a bofom foftened with the leaft degree of humanity. They give us a frightful picture of the effects of defpotic power, guided and inflamed by thofe lufts of the human heart with which it is feldom unaccompanied. Can we forbear weeping for human nature, or blufhing for its degradation, when we view either the fufferer or the actor in fuch a fcene ; the relentlefs oppreffor, or thofe who are " fore broken in the place of dragons ?" What can be more pathetic than the defcription of it

B 2   given

given by the fame Prophet who gave the confolation in our text. "How doth the "city fit folitary that was full of people? "How is fhe become as a widow: fhe that "was great among the nations, and princefs "among the provinces? She weepeth fore "in the night, and her tears are on her "cheeks; fhe hath none to comfort her; "her friends have dealt treacheroufly with "her. Judah is gone into captivity; be- "caufe of affliction, and becaufe of great "fervitude, fhe findeth no reft. Her "mighty men are trodden under foot; "her young men are crufhed; the young "and the old lie on the ground in the "ftreets—Mine eyes do fail with tears; "my bowels are troubled, my liver is "poured on the earth, for the deftruction "of the daughter of my people."

Such are the fruits of lawlefs and defpotic power in a mortal man intoxicated with it: Such defolations does it make in the earth —Such havock in the family of God, merely for the fake of enlarging it's bounds and impreffing its terror on the human bofom. It often, indeed, claims a divine original, and impudently fupports itfelf not barely on the permiffion, but the exprefs defignation of him "whofe tender mercies

are

are over all his works;" though it exactly resembles the grand adversary of God and man, and is only a " roaring lion that seeketh whom he may devour." To plead a divine right for such a power is truly to teach " the doctrine of devils." It covets every thing without bounds : It grasps every thing without pity : It riots on the spoils of innocence and industry : It is proud to annihilate the rights of mankind; to destroy the fairest constitutions of wisdom, policy and justice, the broadest sources of human happiness : While it enslaves the bodies, it debases the minds of the offspring of God : In its progress it changes the very face of nature, it withers even the fruits of the earth, and frustrates the bounties of our common parent. " Before it is the garden of God, behind it is a desolate wilderness."

Looking upon the Jews when groaning under such a power; their armies vanquished; the flower of their country cut off by the sword ; their fortresses reduced ; their cities in ashes ; their land ravaged ; their temple and worship destroyed, and the remnant of the nation led in chains to a foreign land ; who would have thought that in a few years, these cities and this

temple

temple fhould rife again from their ruins, and a people fo totally enflaved and widely difperfed be reftored to their rights and poffeffions, their laws and inftitutions; peace, liberty and plenty daily augmenting their numbers, and lighting up the face of joy through their whole land; while the haughty empire of Babylon, from which they had fuffered fo much, fhould fet to rife no more! Such, however, were the decrees of Heaven; fuch the predictions of the infpired Prophets; and fuch the event.

" Thus faith the Lord of Hofts, I will " break his yoke from off thy neck, and " will burft thy bonds, and ftrangers fhall " no more ferve themfelves of thee; but " thou fhalt ferve the Lord thy God: and " the city fhall be builded upon her own " heap, and they fhall come and fing in " the height of Zion: And fields fhall " be bought in this land whereof ye fay it " is defolate, it is given into the hand of " the Chaldeans—men fhall buy fields for " money. And they that devour thee " fhall be devoured; and they that fpoil " thee fhall be a fpoil. And out of Judah " fhall proceed thankfgiving and the voice " of them that make merry: and I will " multiply them and they fhall not be few;

" I

" I will alfo glorify them and they fhall not
" be fmall. Their children alfo fhall be as
" aforetime, and their congregation, their
" religious and civil affemblies, fhall be
" eftablifhed before me : and I will punifh
" all that opprefs them : and their Nobles
" fhall be of themfelves, and their Gover-
" nor fhall proceed from the midft of
" them, and I will caufe him to draw
" near, and he fhall approach unto me."

When Nebuchadnezzar invaded the land
of Judea, and brought upon it fuch de-
vaftations and miferies, it was governed by
a King, who fhared in the captivity of his
fubjects, and was led with them by the
conqueror in chains to Babylon. But in
the happy reftoration promifed in our text,
it is obfervable, that the royal part of their
government was not to be renewed. No
mention is made in this refrefhing pre-
diction of a King, but only of Nobles,
men of principal character and influence,
who were to *be of themfelves*, and fuch as
they would chufe to conduct their affairs ;
and a Governor, who fhould alfo *proceed
from the midft of them*, and prefide over
all, cloathed with a tempered authority and
dignity, not with arbitary power, and the
means of gratifying an unbounded avarice
and ambition.

The

The form of government originally eftablifhed in the Hebrew nation by a charter
from Heaven, was that of a free republic,
over.which God himfelf, in peculiar favour
to that people, was pleafed to prefide. It
confifted of three parts ; a chief magiftrate
who was called judge or leader, fuch as
Jofhua and others, a council of feventy chofen men, and the general affemblies of the
people. Of thefe the two laft were the
moft effential and permanent, and the firft
more occafional, according to the particular
circumftances of the nation. Their Council
or Sanhedrim, remained with but little fuf-
penfion, through all the viciffitudes they experienced, till after the commencement of
the chriftian æra. And as to the affemblies
of the people, that they were frequently held
by divine appointment, and confidered as the
fountain of civil power, which they exerted
by their own decrees, or diftributed into
various channels as they judged moft conducive to their own fecurity, order, and
happinefs, is evident beyond contradiction
from the facred hiftory. Even the law of
Mofes, though framed by God himfelf, was
not impofed upon that people againft their
will ; it was laid open before the whole
congregation of Ifrael ; they freely adopted
it, and it became their law, not only by
divine

divine appointment, but by their own voluntary and exprefs confent. Upon this account
it is called in the facred writings a *Covenant*,
compaĉt, or mutual ftipulation.

A folemn renewal of this covenant was
the very laft public aĉt of Jofhua their re-
nowned leader. "He gathered all the tribes
of Ifrael to Sechem, and called for the elders
of Ifrael, and for the heads and for the judges, and for their officers, and they prefented
themfelves before God." The occafion was
great and important ; being nothing lefs
than to renew their acceptance of the conftitution they had received from Heaven,
and folemnly to confirm the national compaĉt. How auguft was this affembly of a
great nation, it's reprefentatives and magi-
ftrates of every order, with their brave and
faithful leader at their head ; He, who had
been foremoft to face the dangers of their
caufe, who had fought fo many battles for
their happy fettlement, and rendered fuch
various and important fervices to his country. In a fhort but nervous and pathetic
addrefs to the affembly, he reminded them
of their fmall original ; of the peculiar
favors granted by Heaven to their proge-
nitors ; of their remarkable deliverance
from the flavery of Egypt; of the wonders
wrought for them by a divine hand in their

C   progrefs

progreſs thro' the wilderneſs ; in their con-
queſts on the borders of Canaan, and their
firm poſſeſſion of that promiſed land.
Deeply impreſſed with this intereſting re-
collection, he warmly declares his own reſo-
lution to abide by that noble cauſe for
which they had been led by Heaven from
an ignominious and ſervile dependence,
and formed into a diſtinct and reſpectable
nation. But as the memorable act of the
day depended intirely on the conſent of
the people, he accordingly refers the matter to their own free determination. "Chuſe
you this day whom you will ſerve." It
was impoſſible for the people not to be
moved by ſuch an addreſs ; not to diſcern
the excellency of the moſaic conſtitutions ;
how well they were adapted to the particular circumſtances of the nation, and the
noble purpoſes they were deſigned to pro-
mote. The people replied, *the Lord our
God we will ſerve* ; we conſent, and are
determined to be governed by the laws and
the ſtatutes he has been ſo graciouſly plea-
ſed to afford us. "Then Joſhua ſaid unto
the people, ye are witneſſes againſt yourſelves
that ye have choſen the Lord to ſerve him ;
and they ſaid, we are witneſſes." If ever
we renounce the conſtitution and happy
ſettlement granted to us by Heaven ; if ever
we.

we break the facred compact ; this day, and
all the public and voluntary tranfactions of
it, muft be a witnefs againft us. "Thus
Jofhua made a covenant with the people
at Sechem", which, we are afterwards told,
he recorded in a book, and at the fame
time erected a monumental ftone upon the
foot, as a memorial of thefe facred ftipulations, and as a perpetual teftimony, that the
Supreme Ruler himfelf had not eftablifhed
their polity without their own free concurrence, and that the Hebrew nation, lately redeemed from tyranny, had now a civil
and religious conftitution of their own
choice, and were governed by laws to which
they had given their folemn confent.

To mention all the paffages in facred
writ which prove that the Hebrew government, tho' a theocracy, was yet as to the
outward part of it, a free republic, and
that the fovereignty refided in the people,
would be to recite a large part of it's hiftory. I will therefore only add a fingle in-
ftance. When the tribes of Reuben and
Gad, and the half tribe of Manaffah had
erected a feparate altar, tho' it afterwards
appeared with no bad intention, all the
other tribes were extremely alarmed, and
being met in General Affembly, determined

to make war on their offending brethren.
But previous to the intended affault they
agreed to fend an embaffy to expoftulate with
them on the occafion. Phinehaz and ten
princes, or principal men, were appointed for
this purpofe. Here was an act of fovereignty, and an act of the higheft importance to
the intereft of any nation, involving in it
nothing lefs than the power of making
peace or war. It was not done by Jofhua,
tho' he was then alive; it was an act of the
congregation of Ifrael: The embaffy upon
this momentous matter was chofen, com-
miffioned, and inftructed by them. "As
it was democratically fent, fays a great author, * who wrote conclufively, who fought
bravely, and died glorioufly in the caufe of
liberty, it was democratically received: It
was not directed to one man, but to all
the children of Reuben, Gad and Manaffah, and the anfwer was fent by them all."
The report was made to the congregation,
who finally determined the grand queftion,
and decided for peace.

Such was the civil conftitution of the
Hebrew nation, till growing weary of the
gift of Heaven, they demanded a King.
After being admonifhed by the Prophet
Samuel of the ingratitude and folly of their
request,

* See *Algernon Sidney* upon Government.

requeſt, they were puniſhed in the grant
of it. Impiety, corruption and diſorder of
every kind afterwards increaſing among
them, they grew ripe for the judgments of
Heaven in their deſolation and captivity.
Taught by theſe judgments the value of
thoſe bleſſings they had before deſpiſed, and
groaning under the hand of tyranny more
heavy than that of death, they felt the
worth of their former civil and religious
privileges, and were prepared to receive
with gratitude and joy a reſtoration not
barely to the land flowing with milk and
honey, but to the moſt precious advantage
they ever enjoyed in that land, their original conſtitution of government : They were
prepared to welcome with the voice of
mirth and thankſgiving the re-eſtabliſhment
of their congregations ; nobles choſen from
among themſelves, and a governor proceed-
ing from the midſt of them.

. Such a conſtitution, twice eſtabliſhed by
the hand of Heaven in that nation, ſo far
as it reſpects civil and religious liberty in
general, ought to be regarded as a ſolemn
recognition from the Supreme Ruler himſelf of the rights of human nature. Ab-
ſtracted from thoſe appendages and for-
malities which were peculiar to the Jews,
and

and designed to answer some particular pur-
poses of divine Providence, it points out
in general what kind of government infinite
wisdom and goodness would establish among
mankind.

We want not, indeed, a special revela-
tion from Heaven to teach us that men are
born equal and free ; that no man has a
natural claim of dominion over his neigh-
bours nor one nation any such claim upon
another ; and that as government is only
the administration of the affairs of a number of men combined for their own security
and happiness, such a society have a right
freely to determine by whom and in what
manner their own affairs shall be adminifter-
ed. These are the plain dictates of that
reason and common sense with which the
common parent of men has informed the
human bosom. It is, however, a satisfacti-
on to observe such everlasting maxims of
equity confirmed, and impressed upon the
consciences of men, by the instructions,
precepts, and examples given us in the sa-
cred oracles ; one internal mark of their
divine original, and that they come from
him " who hath made of one blood all
nations to dwell upon the face of the
earth," whose authority sanctifies only those
governments

governments that inſtead of oppreſſing any
part of his family, vindicate the oppreſſed,
and reſtrain and puniſh the oppreſſor.

Unhappy the people who are deſtitute of
the bleſſing promiſed in our text ; who
have not the ulterior powers of government
within themſelves ; who depend upon the
will of another State, with which they are
not incorporated as a vital part, the intereſt
of which muſt in many reſpects be oppoſite
to their own ; and who at the ſame time
have no fixed conſtitutional barrier to reſtrain
this reigning power : There is no mean-
neſs or miſery to which ſuch a people is not
liable : There is not a ſingle bleſſing, tho’
perhaps indulged to them for a while, that
they can call their own ; there is nothing
they have not to dread. Whether the go-
verning power be itſelf free or deſpotic, it
matters not to the poor dependent. Nations who are jealous of their own liberties
often ſport with thoſe of others ; nay, it
has been remarked, that the dependent
provinces of free ſtates have enjoyed leſs
freedom than thoſe belonging to deſpotic
powers. Such was our late diſmal ſituation,
from which Heaven hath redeemed us by
a ſignal and glorious revolution. We
thought, indeed, we had a charter to ſupport

port our rights ; but we found a written charter, a thin barrier againſt all-prevailing power, that could conſtrue it to its own purpoſe, or reſcind it by the ſword at its own pleaſure.

Upon our preſent independence, ſweet and valuable as the bleſſing is, we may read the inſcription, *I am found of them that ſought me not.* Be it to our praiſe or blame, we cannot deny, that when we were not ſearching for it, it happily found us. It certainly muſt have been not only innocent but laudable and manly, to have deſired it even before we felt the abſolute neceſſity of it. It was our birth right ; we ought to have valued it highly, and never to have received a *meſs of pottage,* a ſmall temporary ſupply, as an equivalent for it. Going upon the trite metaphor of a mother country, which has ſo often been weakly urged againſt us, like a child grown to maturity, we had a right to a diſtinct ſettlement in the world, and to the fruits of our own induſtry ; and it would have been but juſtice, and no great generoſity, in her who ſo much boaſted her maternal tenderneſs to us, had ſhe not only readily acquieſced, but even aided us in this ſettlement. It is certain, however, that we did not ſeek

an

an independence; and it is equally certain that Britain, though fhe meant to oppofe it with all her power, has by a ftrange infatuation, taken the moft direct, and perhaps the only methods that could have eftablifhed it. Her oppreffions, her unrelenting cruelty, have driven us out from the family of which we were once a part : This has opened our eyes to difcern the ineftimable bleffing of a feparation from her; while, like children that have been inhumanly treated and caft out by their parents, and at the fame time are capable of taking care of themfelves, we have found friendfhip and refpect from the world, and have formed new, advantageous, and honorable connections.

Independence gives us a rank among the nations of the earth, which no precept of our religion forbids us to underftand and feel, and which we fhould be ambitious to fupport in the moft reputable manner. It opens to us a free communication with all the world, not only for the improvement of commerce, and the acquifition of wealth, but alfo for the cultivation of the moft ufeful knowledge. It naturally unfetters and expands the human mind, and prepares it for the impreffion of the moft exalted vir-

C   tues,

tues, as well as the reception of the moft important fcience. If we look into the hiftory and character of nations, we fhall find thofe that have been for a long time, and to any confiderable degree dependent upon others, limited and cramped in their improvements ; corrupted by the court, and ftained with the vices of the ruling ftate ; and debafed by an air of fervility and depreffion marking their productions and manners. Servility is not only difhonorable to human nature, but commonly accompanied with the meaneft vices, fuch as adulation, deceit, falfhood, treachery, cruelty, and the bafeft methods of fupporting and procuring the favour of the power upon which it depends.

Neither does the time allow, nor circumftances require, that I fhould enter into a detail of all the principles and arguments upon which the right of our prefent eftablifhment is grounded. They are known to all the world; they are to be found in the immortal writings of *Sidney* and *Locke*, and other glorious defenders of the liberties of human nature ; they are alfo to be found, not difhonored, in the acts and publications of America on this great occafion, which have the approbation and applaufe of the wife and impartial among mankind, and

even

even in Britain itfelf : They are the principles upon which her own government.
and her own revolution under William.
the third were founded ; principles which
brutal force may oppofe, but which reafon
and fcripture will forever fanctify. The
citizens of thefe States have had fenfe
enough to comprehend the full force of
thefe principles, and virtue enough, in the
face of uncommon dangers, to act upon fo,
juft, fo broad, and ftable a foundation.

It has been faid, that every nation is
free that deferves to be fo. This may not
be always true : But had a people fo illu-
minated as the inhabitants of thefe States,
fo nurtured by their anceftors in the love of
freedom ; a people to whom divine Providence was pleafed to prefent fo fair an opportunity of afferting their natural right as
an independent nation, and who were even
compelled by the arms of their enemies to
take fanctuary in the temple of Liberty;
had fuch a people been difobedient to the
heavenly call, and refufed to enter, who
could have afferted their title to the glorious wreaths and peculiar bleffings that
are no where beftowed but in that hallowed
place ?

It

It is to the dishonor of human nature, that Liberty, wherever it has been planted and flourished, has commonly required to be watered with blood. Britain, in her conduct towards these States, hath given a fresh proof of the truth of this observation. She has attempted to destroy by her arms in America, what she professes to defend by these very arms on her own soil. Such is the nature of man, such the tendency of power in a nation as well as a single person. It makes a perpetual effort to enlarge itself, and presses against the bounds that confine it. It loses by degrees all idea of right but its own; and therefore that people must be unhappy indeed, who have nothing but humble petitions and re-monstrances, and the feeble voice of a charter to oppose to the arms of another nation, that claims A RIGHT TO BIND THEM IN ALL CASES WHATSOEVER.

Poor Genoa! says an author* who exposes with great energy and spirit the idea of re-ceiving as the gift of a despot, by a written charter, a title to the rights of human nature, and to which all men are born; " Poor Genoa! wherefore shouldest thou be vain of exhibiting a charter of privileges given thee by one Berenger : Concessions of privileges

* Voltaire.

leges are but titles of servitude: The true Charter of Liberty is *Independency supported by Force.*—It is with the point of the sword the diplomas that ratify this natural right must be signed. Happy Switzerland! To what placart owest thou thy Liberty? To thy courage, thy firmness, thy mountains. But hold——— I am your Emperor. " We do not chuse you should be any longer so." But your fathers were my father's slaves. " It is for that reason their children will not be your's." But I have a right by dignity.— " And we have a right by nature. When did the Seven United Provinces become possessed of this incontestable right? From the moment they united; and from that moment Philip II. became the Rebel."

Heaven and *earth* can bear witness that these States are innocent of the blood that hath been shed, and the miseries diffused by this unrighteous war. We have stood upon the ground of justice, honor, and liberty, and acted meerly a defensive part. Not unreasonable in our demands, not violent in our councils, not precipitate in our conduct, our " moderation has been known to all men;" and without refusing a single claim that Britain could in equity make

make upon us, our perfons, our property,
our rights have been invaded in every
ftep that led to this revolution. I do
not wifh that this fhould be taken for
granted barely upon our own declaration.
Without appealing to foreign nations,
whofe conduct towards us demonftrates
what opinion they form of our principles
and meafures; we have an acknowledgment of the truth of this affertion from
Britain itfelf; from men of approved
wifdom, integrity and candor; from fome
of the firft characters, and brighteft orna-
ments in her own government; from innumerable fpeeches in her Parliaments,
and from folemn protefts in her Houfe
of Lords.

Allow me particularly to mention on
this occafion the letters of Mr. HARTLEY,
member of the Britifh Houfe of Commons
for Hull, to his conftituents; in which he
gives a detail of the meafures of that
government refpecting America, and upon
which he fays;—" Thinking, as I have
always thought, that the FOUNDATION
and PROSECUTION of the war againft
America has been unjuft, I have taken
fome pains to lay open thofe infidious
arts which minifters have practifed, that I
may

may contribute my. feeble efforts to vindicate my country at large from fo grie-
vous a charge as that of fupporting an
unjuft caufe, knowing it to be unjuft."
In another place, he fays, " When all
thofe tranfactions fhall come hereafter to
to be revifed in fome cooler hour, I am
confident there is not a man with a Britifh
heart who will not fay, that in the fame
circumftances he would have acted as the
Americans have done." He goes on,
" What had the Americans to look to
after the refufal of their laft petition, but
to feek for fhelter in their own ftrength
and Independence? They were cut off
from all poffible communication with their
fovereign and their mother country; and
the firft act of the fecond feffion of parliament was to caft them out of all national and parliamentary protection; to
fend 20,000 German mercenaries againft
them; to incite an infurrection of negroes
againft their mafters, and to let loofe the
Indian Savages upon their innocent and
unarmed back fettlers, and upon defencelefs
women and children. They had peti-
tioned and addreffed; they had difclaimed
every idea of independence; in return for
which adminiftration. fends againft them an
army of 50,000 men. Now let minifters
anfwer

anſwer to God and their country for the
blood which they have ſhed. The blood
of thouſands of their fellow creatures,
wilfully and premeditatedly ſhed in an un-
juſt cauſe, will be required at their hands ;
who have taken their full ſtretch of ven-
geance, in their attempts to deſtroy and
to lay waſte to the utmoſt of their ma-
lignant power the lives, liberty, property,
and all the rights of mankind."

Nothing can be more full to the point
than this acknowledgment from a gentle-
man of ſuch diſtinguiſhed character : He
imputes indeed the whole to the miniſters,
but as it was all adopted and authoriſed
by the whole Britiſh government, it became
an act of the nation in general ; though
many worthy individuals, with himſelf,
abhorred the injuſtice and cruelty.

In the proteſt of the Lords, againſt the
prohibitory bill, the diſſentient Peers ſay,
" We are preparing the minds of the
Americans for that Independence we charge
them with affecting, whilſt we drive them
to the *neceſſity* of it by repeated injuries."
" I rejoice that the Americans have re-
ſiſted," ſaid Lord Chatham in parliament ;
a ſhort but full teſtimony from that great

man

man to the juftice of our caufe.

Thus are we acquitted from the guilt of all
this blood that " crieth from the ground,"
by the public declarations of many of the
wifeft and beft men in Britain ; men who per-
fectly knew all the meafures of her government, and all that could be offered to
juftify them, being themfelves a part of this
government : Men deeply verfed in natural
and political law, capable of forming the
trueft judgment upon fo important a point,
and who cannot be fufpected of partiality in
our favour. With all this juftice on our fide,
we ftill put our caufe to great hazard by de-
laying to declare ourfelves a feperate nation,
even after Britain had with her own hands
violently broken every bond of union.

By this conduct of our enemies, Heaven
hath granted us an ineftimable opportunity,
and fuch as has been rarely if ever indulged to fo great a people : An opportunity
to avail ourfelves of the wifdom and experience of all paft ages united with that of
the prefent ; of comparing what we have
feen and felt ourfelves, with what we have
known and read of others ; and of chufing for ourfelves, unencumbered with the
pretenfions

pretenfions of royal heirs, or lordly peers, of feudal rights, or ecclefiaftical authority, that form of civil government which we judge moft conducive to our own fecurity and order, liberty and happinefs : An opportunity, though furrounded with the flames of war, of deliberating and deciding upon this moft interefting of all human affairs with calmnefs and freedom. ' This, in all it's circumftances, is a fingular event ; it is hard to tell where another fuch fcene was ever beheld. The origin of moft nations is covered with obfcurity, and veiled by fiction ; the rife of our own is open as it is honorable ; and the new-born ftate, may I not be allowed to fay, is a " fpecta-cle to men and angels". For as piety; virtue, and morals are not a little interefted in government, fuch a tranfaction has an afpect upon both worlds ; and concerns us not only as members of civil fociety upon earth, but as candidates for "the city of the living God, the Jerufalem on high".

Happy people! who not awed by the voice of a mafter ; not chained by flavifh cuftoms, fuperftitions, and prejudices, have deliberately framed the conftitution under which you chufe to live ; and are to be

fubject

subject to no laws, by which you do not consent to bind yourselves. In such an attitude human nature appears with it's proper dignity: On such a basis, life, and all that sweetens and adorns it, may rest with as much security as human imperfection can possibly admit: In such a constitution we find a country deserving to be loved, and worthy to be defended. For what is our country? Is it a soil of which, tho' we may be the present possessors, we can call no part our own? or the air in which we first drew our breath, from which we may be confined in a dungeon, or of which we may be deprived by the ax or the halter at the pleasure of a tyrant? Is not a country a constitution—an established frame of laws; of which a man may say, "we are here united in society for our common security and happiness. These fields and these fruits are my own: The regulations under which I live are my own; I am not only a proprietor in the soil, but I am part of the sovereignty of my country". Such ought to be the community of men, and such, adored be the goodness of the supreme Ruler of the world, such, at present is our own country; of which this day affords a bright evidence, a glorious recognition.   E 2   To

To the difappointment of our enemies, and the joy of our friends, we have now attained a fettled government with a degree of peace and unanimity, all circumftances confidered, truly furprizing. The fagacity, the political knowledge, the patient deliberation, the conftant attention to the grand principles of liberty, and the mutual condefcention and candor under a diverfity of apprehenfion refpecting the modes of adminiftration, exhibited by thofe who were appointed to form this conftitution, and by the people who ratified it, muft do immortal honor to our country. It is, we believe, "an happy foundation for many generations" ; and the framers of it are indeed the *Fathers* of their country ; fince nothing is fo effential to the increafe, and univerfal profperity of a community, as a conftitution of government founded in juftice, and friendly to liberty. Such men have a monument of glory more durable than brafs or marble.

I need not enlarge before fuch an audience upon the particular excellencies of this conftitution : How effectually it makes the people the keepers of their own liberties, with whom they are certainly fafeft : How nicely it poizes the powers of government,

ment, in order to render them as far as
human forefight can, what God ever defigned they fhould be, powers only to do
good : How happily it guards on the one
hand againft anarchy and confufion, and
on the other againft tyranny and oppreffion : How carefully it feparates the legifla-
tive from the executive power, a point effential to liberty : How wifely it has pro-
vided for the impartial execution of the
laws in the independent fituation of the
judges ; a matter of capital moment, and
without which the freedom of a conftitution in other refpects, might be often de-
lufory, and not realized in the juft fecurity
of the perfon and property of the fubject.

In addition to all this, what a broad
foundation for the exercife of the rights of
confcience is laid in this conftitution! which
declares, that " no fubject fhall be hurt, mo-
lefted, or reftrained in his perfon, liberty
or eftate, for worfhipping God in the manner and feafon moft agreeable to the dictates of his own confcience, or for his religious profeffion or fentiments ; and that
every denomination of chriftians, demean-
ing themfelves peaceably, and as good fubjects of the commonwealth, fhall be equally
                                    under

under the protection of the law, and no
fubordination of any one fect or denomination to another fhall be eftablifhed by
law." It confiders indeed morality and
the public worfhip of God as important to
the happinefs of fociety : And furely it
would be an affront to the people of this
ftate, as the convention fpeak in their previous addrefs, "to labor to convince them
that the honor and happinefs of a people
depend upon morality ; and that the public worfhip of God has a tendency to in-
culcate the principles thereof, as well as to
preferve a people from forfaking civilization,
and falling into a ftate of favage barbarity".

Of thefe, and other excellent properties
of our prefent conftitution, the citizens of
this ftate are throughly fenfible, or well informed, and jealous as they are of their
rights, they never would have adopted and
ratified it with fo great a degree of unanimity. They know it is framed upon an
extent of civil and religious liberty, unex-
ampled perhaps in any country in the world,
except America. This muft highly endear
it to them ; and while it is written upon
their own hearts, they have the fatisfaction
to find that it has already received the elo-
giums

giums of others, whofe capacity and diftinction render their teftimony truly honorable.
But left thro' the imperfection of human
nature, and after all the deliberation and
caution with which it has been formed and
approved, fome inconveniences fhould be
found lurking in it, of which experience
can beft inform us, a right is exprefsly re-
ferved to the people of removing them in
a revifion of the whole, after a fair experi-
ment of fifteen years.

When a people have the rare felicity
of chufing their own government, every
part of it fhould firft be weighed in the
balance of reafon, and nicely adjufted to
the claims of liberty, equity and order ;
but when this is done, a warm and paffion-
ate patriotifm fhould be added to the refult
of cool deliberation, to put in motion and
animate the whole machine. The citizens
of a free republic fhould reverence their
conftitution : They fhould not only calmly
approve, and readily fubmit to it, but regard it alfo with veneration and affection
rifing even to an enthufiafm, like that which
prevailed at Sparta and at Rome. Nothing
can render a commonwealth more illuftrious, nothing more powerful, than fuch a
manly

manly, fuch a facred fire. Every thing
will then be fubordinated to the public
welfare ; every labour neceffary to this will
be chearfully endured, every expence readily fubmitted to, every danger boldly con-
fronted.

May this heavenly flame animate all
orders of men in the ftate ! May it catch
from bofom to bofom, and the glow be
univerfal ! May a double portion of it in-
habit the breafts of our civil rulers, and
impart a luftre to them like that which fat
upon the face of Mofes, when he came
down from the holy mountain with the
tables of the Hebrew conftitution in his
hand ! Thus will they fuftain with true
dignity the firft honours, the firft marks of
efteem and confidence, the firft public em-
ployments beftowed by this new commonwealth, and in which they this day appear.
Such men muft naturally care for our
ftate ; men whofe abilities and virtues have
obtained a fanction from the free fuffrages
of their enlightned and virtuous fellow
citizens. Are not thefe fuffrages, a public
and folemn teftimony that in the opinion
of their conftituents, they are men who
have fteadily acted upon the noble principles

ples on which the frame of our government now refts?—Men who have gene-
roufly neglected their private intereft in an
ardent purfuit of that of the public—Men
who have intrepidly oppofed one of the
greateft powers on earth, and put their
fortunes and their lives to no fmall hazard
in fixing the bafis of our freedom and
honour. Who can forbear congratulating
our rifing State, and cafting up a thankful
eye to Heaven, upon this great and fingular occafion, the eftablifhment of our
Congregation; our Nobles freely chofen
by ourfelves; and our Governour coming
forth, at the call of his country, from the
midft of us?

Behold the man, whofe name as Prefident
of Congrefs, authenticates that immortal
act, which, in form, conftitutes the Independence of thefe United States, and by
which *a nation* was literally *born in a day!*
See Him, who had taken too early and
decided a part, and done too much for the
liberties of America, to be forgiven by
it's enemies! See Him, whofe name, with
that of another diftinguifhed patriot,* was
exprefsly excepted from a Britifh act of
grace, and upon whofe head a price was

F　　virtually

* The Honorable Samuel Adams, Efq;

virtually bid by thofe who meant to en-
flave us : Behold this very man, declared
by the voice of his country, " the head of
the corner" in our political building ; the
firft Magiftrate of this free Commonwealth.
It was not in the power of his fellow-
citizens to give an higher teftimony how
well they remember the generous and
important fervices he has already rendered
to his country, and how much they con-
fide in his difpofition and abilities ftill to
ferve it.

May God Almighty take his Excellency
and the other honourable branches of the
government, the Lieutenant-Governour, the
Council, the Senate, and Houfe of Reprefentatives into his holy protection, and
unite them in meafures glorious to themfelves, and happy to their country ! Vefted
as they are with particular honours, they
have a painful preheminence : Their dif-
tinctions call them to the moft weighty and
important cares, at a time when the adminiftration of public affairs is attended with
peculiar difficulties. They need therefore
the gracious direction and affiftance of the
" bleffed and only Potentate." which, in
this folemn affembly of rulers and people,
we jointly and devoutly implore.

The

The people of a free State have a right
to expect from thofe whom they have
honoured with the direction of their public
concerns, a faithful and unremitting attention to thefe concerns. He who accepts
a public truft, pledges himfelf, his facred
honour, and by his official oath appeals to
his God, that with all good fidelity, and to
the utmoft of his capacity he will difcharge
this truft. And that Commonwealth which
doth not keep an eye of care upon thofe
who govern, and obferve how they behave
in their feveral departments, in order to
regulate its fuffrages upon this ftandard, will
foon find itfelf in perplexity, and cannot
expect long to preferve either its dignity or
happinefs.

Dignity of conduct is ever connected
with the happinefs of a State ; particularly
at its rife, and the firft appearance it makes
in the world. Then all eyes are turned
upon it ; they view it with attention ; and
the firft impreffions it makes are commonly
lafting. This circumftance muft render
the conduct of our prefent rulers peculiarly
important, and fall with particular weight
upon their minds. We hope from their
wifdom and abilities, their untainted integrity and unfhaken firmnefs, this new

F 2   formed

formed Commonwealth will rife with honour
and applaufe, and attract that refpect, which
the number and quality of its inhabitants,
the extent of its territory and commerce,
and the natural advantages with which it
is bleft, cannot fail, under a good government, to command.

From our prefent happy eftablifhment
we may reafonably hope for a new energy
in government; an energy that fhall be
felt in all parts of the State: We hope
that the finews of civil authority through
its whole frame will be well braced, and
the public intereft in all its extended
branches be well attended to ; that no
officer will be permitted to negleft the
                    tranfgrefs the bounds of his de-
                    that peculations, frauds, and
en   mailer oppreffions in any office,
v   tfully prevented, or exempla-
                    that no corruption will
                to reft in any part of the
            no not in the extremeft,
                    pread by degrees, and finally
                    ury vitals of the community.

        nefs, fays one of the greateft
        d wifeft princes that ever lived,
        nefs exalteth a nation." This
                                maxim

maxim doth not barely reft upon his own
but alfo on a divine authority ; and the
truth of it hath been verified by the experience of all ages.

Our civil rulers will remember, that as
piety and virtue fupport the honour and happinefs of every community, they are peculiarly requifite in a free government: Virtue
is the fpirit of a Republic ; for where all
power is derived from the people, all depends on their good difpofition. If they
are impious, factious and felfifh ; if they are
abandoned to idlenefs, diffipation, luxury,
and extravagance ; if they are loft to the
fear of God, and the love of their country,
all is loft. Having got beyond the re-
ftraints of a divine authority, they will not
brook the control of laws enacted by rulers
of their own creating. We may therefore
rely that the prefent Government will do
all it fairly can, by authority and example,
to anfwer the end of its inftitution, that the
members of this Commonwealth may *lead
a quiet and peaceable life in all.* GODLI-
NESS as well as *honefty*, and our liberty
never be juftly reproached as licentioufnefs.

I know there is a diverfity of fentiment
refpecting the extent of civil power in religious

gious matters. Inftead of entering into the difpute, may I be allowed from the warmth of my heart, to recommend, where confcience is pleaded on both fides, mutual candour and love, and an happy union of all denominations in fupport of a government, which though human, and therefore not abfolutely perfect, is yet certainly founded on the broadeft bafis of liberty, and affords equal protection to all. Warm parties upon civil or religious matters, or from perfonal confiderations, are greatly injurious to a free State, and particularly fo to one newly formed. We have indeed lefs of this than might be expected: We fhall be happy to have none at all; happy indeed, when every man fhall love and ferve his country, and have that fhare of public influence and refpect, without diftinction of parties, which his virtues and fervices may juftly demand. This is the true fpirit of a Commonwealth, centring all hearts, and all hands in the common intereft.

Neither piety, virtue, or liberty can long flourifh in a community, where the education of youth is neglected. How much do we owe to the care of our venerable anceftors upon this important object? Had not they laid fuch foundations for
training

training up their children in knowledge
and religion, in science, and arts, should
we have been so respectable a community
as we this day appear? Should we have
understood our rights so clearly? or valued
them so highly? or defended them with
such advantage? Or should we have been
prepared to lay that basis of liberty, that
happy constitution, on which we raise
such large hopes, and from which we
derive such uncommon joy? We may
therefore be confident that the schools,
and particularly the university, founded
and cherished by our wise and pious
fathers, will be patronized and nursed by
a government which is so much indebted
to them for its honour and efficacy, and
the very principles of its existence. The
present circumstances of those institutions
call for the kindest attention of our rulers;
and their close connection with every public
interest, civil and religious, strongly en-
forces the call.

The sciences and arts, for the encou-
ragement of which a new foundation*
hath lately been laid in this Commonwealth,
deserve the countenance and particular
favour of every government. They are
not only ornamental but useful: They not
only

* The American Academy of Arts and Sciences.

only polifh, but fupport, enrich, and defend a community. As they delight in
liberty, they are particularly friendly to
free States. Barbarians are fierce and un-
governable, and having the groffeft ideas
of order, and the benefits refulting from
it, they require the hand of a ftern mafter;
but a people enlightened and civilized by
the fciences and liberal arts, have fentiments that fupport liberty and good laws:
They may be guided by a filken thread;
and the mild punifhments proper to a free
State are fufficient to guard the public
peace.

An eftablifhed honour and fidelity in
all public engagements and promifes, form
a branch of righteoufnefs that is wealth,
is power, and fecurity to a State : It pre-
vents innumerable perplexities : It creates
confidence in the government from fubjects and from ftrangers: It facilitates the
moft advantageous connections : It extends
credit; and eafily obtains fupplies in the
moft preffing public emergencies, and when
nothing elfe can obtain them : While the
want of it, whatever benefits fome fhort-
fighted politicians may have promifed from
delufive expedients, and deceitful arts, ren-
ders a State weak and contemptible; ftrips
it

it of its defence; grieves and provoke its
friends, and delivers it up to the will of its
enemies. Upon what does the power of
the Britiſh nation chiefly reſt at this moment ? That power that has been ſo un-
righteouſly employed againſt America ?
Upon the long and nice preſervation of her
faith in all monied matters. With all her
injuſtice in other inſtances, meer policy hath
obliged her to maintain a fair character
with her creditors. The ſupport this hath
given her in frequent and expenſive wars,
by the ſupplies it has enabled her to raiſe
upon loan, is aſtoniſhing. By this her
government hath availed itſelf of the whole
immenſe capital of the national debt,
which hath been expended in the public
ſervice; while the creditors content themſelves with the bare payment of the intereſt. It may be demonſtrated that the
growing reſources of theſe ſtates, under
the conduct of prudence and juſtice, are
ſufficient to form a fund of credit for pro-
ſecuting the preſent war, ſo ruinous to
Britain, much longer than that nation,
loaded as ſhe now is, can poſſibly ſupport it.

But need I urge, in a chriſtian audience,
and before chriſtian rulers, the importance
of preſerving inviolate the public faith !

If

If this is allowed to be important at all times, and to all ftates, it muft be peculiarly fo to thofe whofe. foundations are newly laid, and who are but juft numbered among the nations of the earth. They have a national chara&er to eftablifh, upon which their very exiftence may depend. Shall we not then rely that the prefent government will employ every meafure in their power, to maintain in this commonwealth a clear juftice, an untainted honour in all public engagements ; in all laws refpe&ing property ; in all regulations of taxes ; in all our conduct towards our fifter ftates, and towards our allies abroad.

The treaty of alliance and friendfhip between HIS MOST CHRISTIAN MAJESTY and thefe ftates, is engraved on every bofom friendly to the rights and independence of America. If fidelity dwells in fuch bofoms, it will be confpicuous on every occafion of performing our own part of thefe facred ftipulations. The intereft is indeed mutual, as was openly confeffed : The treaty is therefore natural, and likely to be lafting. But mutual intereft doth not always banifh generofity ; a proof of which our illuftriousAlly hath given in this compa& ; a proof not unapplauded in Europe, tho' particular-

ly

ly felt and acknowledged in America. I
will not affront either the underftanding or
the feelings of this refpectable audience, by
attempting formally to demonftrate that we
have received great advantages and fupport
from this friendfhip. It is impoffible we
fhould forget the firft pledge of it, in the
fquadron fent to our aid under the orders
of that vigilant, active and intrepid commander the COUNT D'ESTAING ; who
greatly difconcerted the defigns of the ene-
my, and did every thing for us that wifdom
and valour, in his fituation, could perform.
Nor need I call your attention to that important armament lately arrived to our
affiftance, under leaders of diftinguifhed
abilities, and the moft eftablifhed military
reputation. France, tho' a monarchy, has
been the nurfe and protectrefs of free re-
publics. Switzerland among others can
atteft to this : Her free States can atteft,
that during an alliance with France of more
than three hundred years, their liberties
have been conftantly befriended by that
nation, and every part of the treaty for
their fupport punctually performed. This
they have acknowledged in a late folemn
renewal of the alliance. An happy omen
to thefe States, whofe circumftances are in
many refpects fimilar to thofe of the united
cantons of Switzerland.

The perfonal and royal accomplifhments of LOUIS THE SIXTEENTH are known and admired far beyond his own extended dominions, and afford the brighteft profpect to his fubjects and allies. The reign of this monarch diffufes new fpirit through his kingdom, and gives frefhnefs to the glory of France. A Britifh author, in his account of the regulations which took place after this prince had afcended the throne, calls him "a paternal and patriotic fovereign, who wherever he appears is loaded with the bleffings of his fubjects." The celebrated Mr. Burke, in his fpeech before the Britifh Houfe of Commons on February laft, adds his own teftimony to this, when fpeaking of fome reforms in the finances and the court of France, he fays, " The minifter who does thefe things is a great man but the prince who defires they fhould be done, is a far greater : We muft do juftice to our enemies ; thefe are the acts of a PATRIOT KING". The friendfhip of fuch a monarch muft be valuable indeed !

The other great and powerful branch of the houfe of Bourbon, the king of Spain, tho' not at prefent formally allied to us, is yet evidently engaged in our caufe, by the union of his arms with thofe of France. We

We cannot be wanting in the sentiments due to the amity and aid of so respectable a potentate. May God Almighty bless these Princes, and their dominions ; and crown their arms, and those of America, with such success as may soon restore to a bleeding world the blessings of peace !

Peace, peace, we ardently wish ; but not upon terms dishonourable to ourselves, or dangerous to our liberties ; and our enemies seem not yet prepared to allow it upon any other. At present the voice of providence, the call of our still invaded country, and the cry of every thing dear to us, all unite to rouze us to prosecute the war with redoubled vigour ; upon the success of which all our free constitutions, all our hopes depend. I need not enumerate the former or more recent events of the war, and the favours or chastisements of heaven sent to us in these events : They are known to you ; they cannot be forgotten : God grant they may be properly improved ! Thro' his aid, amidst all our mistakes and errors, we have already done great things ; but our warfare is not yet accomplished : And our rulers, we hope, like the Roman General, will think nothing done, while any thing remains undone.

We

We have depended too much upon partial meafures, temporary expedients, fhort and interrupted efforts made only upon the fpur of the occafion. An army eftablifhed in proper numbers, for the whole duration of the war, and feafonably furnifhed with all neceffary fupplies, is now univerfally acknowledged of the utmoft confequence to the liberties of America. Particular attention will certainly be paid to the recommendations of this great object from the Commander in chief—that illuftrious man, formed by heaven for the important truft he fuftains, and to draw to a point the confidence of thefe free ftates, and a patriotic army. Part of the gladnefs of this day rifes from the general expectation, that our new government will give new vigour to the meafures neceffary to this momentous purpofe ; that thefe meafures will be inftantly purfued, and without that delay we have too much experienced in times paft ; and which, at this feafon, muft prove greatly diftreffing, if not fatal to our country.

Can we hefitate a moment at the burden and expence ? It is impoffible. Why have the citizens of America been framing fuch wife and excellent conftitutions, if they meant not to maintain, but leave them to become the fport of their enemies ? If after all the

memorable

memorable, things we have done to repel
lawlefs power, and eftablifh our rights ; if
after all we have endured in a war
favagely conducted by our enemies ; if
after the rank we have taken, and the reputation we have acquired as an independent
nation, we fhould now relax in our efforts,
and fuffer tyranny finally to prevail, who
can bear to think of the confequences, or
to look upon the picture imagination prefents ? In fuch a reverfe, we may write
upon this fair region the infcription given
to an antient dungeon.—"You who enter
here, leave behind you every hope". What
would not this people do ; what exertions
would they not make, rather than fubmit to
fuch debafement and mifery ? It is with
you, our civil fathers, to direct fuch a fpirit,
and fuch exertions, in a manner the moft
effectual to the falvation of our country.

What heroes have bled, what invaluable
lives have been offered up to redeem us
from flavery, and place us on a free conftitution ? Their names will never die : Their
honours will never wither. Among thefe we
fee a WARREN, and a MONTGOME*Y :
Liberty wept over their tombs ; and there
would have remained inconfolate, had fhe
not beheld a fucceffion of patriots and
warriors

warriors rifing in the fame fpirit. Rights
retrieved with fuch blood as hath flowed
from the veins of America in our great
caufe, muft certainly be held by us at an
ineftimable price, and improved to the
greateft advantage ; nor can any thing fhew
their value in a clearer light, than a good
adminiftration of our free governments.

Our prefent rulers, as principal founders
of the conftitution, cannot but regard it
with parental tendernefs. They cannot
but love their own offspring, efpecially
when it has features and charms to attract
the love and admiration of the world :
And hoping that their names and their
glory may long live in fuch an offspring,
they have an irrefiftible motive to guard
againft every thing that may weaken or
deform it ; every thing that may render its
exiftence fhort, precarious, or difhonourable.

The fame kind of motive muft excite ·
the body of the people to the fame care.
It is with you alfo my fellow-citizens, by
whofe appointment this conftitution was
framed, and who have folemnly acknowledged it to be your own ; it is with you
to give life and vigour to all its limbs
frefhnefs and beauty to its whole com-
plexion ; to guard it from dangers ; to
preferve

preferve it " from the corruption that is in the world ;" and to produce it upon the great theatre of nations with advantage and glory. We have now a government free indeed ; but after all, it remains with the people, under God, to make it an honourable and happy one : This muft ultimately depend upon the prudence of their elections, and the virtue of their conduct. A government framed by ourfelves for our own benefit, and according to the faireft models of our own minds, and adminiftred by men of our own choice, ought to be more deeply refpected, and more religiously fupported by us than any kind of impofed authority. Having defined and adjufted its powers by our own decifions, and made thofe who are vefted with fuch as are improper to be long continued in the fame hands, amenable, at fhort intervals, to the judgment of the people, we never can allow it too much weight and energy ; we only fupport ourfelves in fupporting fuch authority : While to oppofe or weaken it, or bring it under an undue influence, is with the hand of a parricide to deftroy order, liberty, and happinefs. Upon this general principle, and to eftablifh a dignity and independence, where they muft forever operate to the benefit of the community,

H   the

the citizens of this State have by their prefent Conftitution, moft freely and wifely
fecured to their chief Magiftrate, and the
Juftices of the fupreme judicial Court, permanent and honourable falaries ; an article
which, we cannot doubt, will be facredly
obferved in the true fpirit of theConftitution.

In a word, if the Rulers and the People
act throughout in this fpirit ; if they mu-
tually watch over and fuftain each other ;
and thofe virtues are cultivated among us
which fupport and are fupported by a free
Republic, our new Government will then
open with the moft happy omens, and the
commencement of it will be the æra of our
rifing felicity and glory.

While we receive in the fettlement of
our Commonwealth a reward of our at-
chievements and fufferings, we have the
further confolation to reflect, that they
have tended to the general welfare, and
the fupport of the rights of mankind.
The ftruggle of America hath afforded to
oppreffed Ireland a favourable opportunity
of infifting upon her own privileges : Nor
do any of the powers in Europe oppofe
our caufe, or feem to wifh it may be
unfuccefstul. Britain has maintained her
naval

naval fuperiority with fuch marks of haughtinefs and oppreffion as have juftly given umbrage to the nations around her : They cannot therefore but wifh to fee her power confined within reafonable bounds, and fuch as may be confiftent with the fafety of their own commercial rights. This, they know would at leaft be exceeding diffi- cult, fhould the rapidly increafing force of thefe States be reunited with Britain, and wielded by her, as it hath been in time paft, againft every nation upon whom fhe is pleafed to make war. So favourable, through the divine furperintendence, is the prefent fitu- ation of the powers in Europe, to the liber- ties and independence for which we are contending. But as individuals muft part with fome natural liberties for the fake of the fecurity and advantages of fociety ; the fame kind of commutation muft take place in the great republic of nations. The rights of Kingdoms and States have their bounds ; and as in our own eftablifhment we are not likely to find reafon, I truft we fhall never have an inclination to exceed thefe bounds, and juftly to excite the jealoufy and oppo- fition of other nations. It is thus wifdom, moderation and found policy would connect Kingdoms and States for their mutual advan- tage, and preferve the order and harmony

of

of the world. In all this thefe free States
will find their own fecurity, and rife by
natural and unenvied degrees to that emi-
nence, for which, I would fain perfwade
myfelf, we are defigned.

It is laudable to lay the foundations of
our Republicks with extended views. Rome
rofe to empire becaufe fhe early thought
herfelf deftined for it. The great object
was continually before the eyes of her fons:
It enlarged and invigorated their minds; it
excited their vigilance ; it elated their courage, and prepared them to embrace toils
and dangers, and fubmit to every regulation
friendly to the freedom and profperity of
Rome. They did great things becaufe they
believed themfelves capable, and born to do
them. They reverenced themfelves and
their country; and animated with unbounded refpect for it, they every day added to
its ftrength and glory. Conqueft is not indeed the aim of thefe rifing States; found
policy muft ever forbid it : We have before
us an object more truly great and honourable. We feem called by heaven to make
a large portion of this globe a feat of knowledge and liberty, of agriculture, commerce,
and arts, and what is more important than
all, of chriftian piety and virtue. A celebrated

brated Britifh hiftorian obferves, if I well
remember, that the natural features of America are peculiarly ftriking. Our mountains, our rivers and lakes have a fingular
air of dignity and grandeur. May our
conduct correfpond to the face of our country! At prefent an immenfe part of it lies as
nature hath left it, and human labour and
art have done but little; and brightened only
fome fmall fpecks of a continent that can
afford ample means of fubfiftence to many,
many millions of the human race. It remains with us and our pofterity, to " make
the wildernefs become a fruitful field, and
the defert bloffom as the rofe ;" to eftablifh
the honour and happinefs of this new world,
as far as it may be juftly our own, and to
invite the injured and oppreffed, the worthy
and the good to thefe fhores, by the moft
liberal governments, by wife political inftitutions, by cultivating the confidence and
friendfhip of other nations, and by a facred
attention to that gofpel that breaths " peace
on earth, and good will towards men."
Thus will our country refemble the new
city which St. John faw " coming down
from God out of heaven, adorned as a bride
for her hufband." Is there a benevolent
fpirit on earth, or on high, whom fuch a
profpect would not delight?

But

But what are thofe illuftrious forms that feem to hover over us on the prefent great occafion, and to look down with pleafure on the memorable tranfactions of this day? Are they not the founders and lawgivers, the fkilful pilots and brave defenders of free States, whofe fame " flows down through all ages, enlarging as it flows"? They, who thought no toils or vigilance too great to eftablifh and protect the rights of human nature; no riches too large to be exchanged for them; no blood too precious to be fhed for their redemption?——But who are they who feem to approach nearear to us, and in whofe countenances we difcern a peculiar mixture of gravity and joy upon this folemnity? Are they not the venerable Fathers of the Maffachufetts; who though not perfect while they dwelt in flefh, were yet greatly diftinguifhed by an ardent piety, by all the manly virtues, and by an unquenchable love of liberty——They, who to form a retreat for it, croffed the ocean, through innumerable difficulties, to a favage land: They, who brought with them a broad Charter of Liberty, over which they wept when it was wrefted from them by the hand of power, and an infidious one placed in its room. With

what

what pleafure do they feem to behold
their children, like the antient feed of
Abraham, this day reftored to their original foundations of freedom ! their Governor " as at the firft, and their Coun-
cellors as at the beginning" ? Do they
not call upon us to defend thefe foucda-
tions at every hazard, and to perpetuate
their honour in the liberty and virtue of
the State they planted ?

O thou fupreme Governor of the world,
whofe arm hath done great things for us,
eftablifh the foundations of this Commonwealth, and evermore defend it with the
faving ftrength of thy right hand ! Grant
that here the divine conftitutions of Jefus
thy Son may ever be honoured and maintained ! Grant that it may be the refi-
dence of all private and, patriotic virtues,
of all that enlightens and fupports, all that
fweetens and adorns human fociety, till
the ftates and kingdoms of this world
fhall be fwallowed up in thine own kingdom : In that, which alone is immortal,
may we obtain a perfect citizenfhip, and
enjoy in its completion, " the glorious
Liberty of the Sons of God !——And
let all the people fay, AMEN!

www.ingramcontent.com/pod-product-compliance
Lightning Source LLC
Chambersburg PA
CBHW031749090426
42739CB00008B/945